D1135375

An absolute gem! This book invites us to be stargazers and focus on Jesus, 'the bright morning star'. Against the backdrop of our own despair and the darkness of our world, Jesus is 'the brightest and the best'. As we prepare for Christmas and the New Year, through the lines of carols and rich theology, each day of the devotional offers us comfort, strength and most important of all, the hope of redemption. Like the Magi, our response is worship. This is a book I will be buying and giving to friends.

Elizabeth McQuoid
Commissioning editor, Keswick Ministries

This book is a gift! Its melody line will aid in tuning your heart to the expectant arrival of Christ. The poetry of multiple chapters will help you feel the truth of the incarnation and its implications set to rhythm. The prose Wilson adds will guide you through the Advent season, helping you see the bright richness it offers the people of God who today await Christ's glorious return.

Matthew Boswell
Pastor-hymnwriter, The Trails Church, Celina/Prosper, Texas
Assistant Professor of Christian Music and Worship,
The Southern Baptist Theological Seminary, Louisville, Kentucky

In all the school nativity readings and over-sung carols, Christmas can become a mere nostalgia trip. Many Decembers pass; yet swamped under shepherd's costumes, mince-pies, and wrapping paper, we miss the magnitude of the incarnation completely. In this book Philippa Ruth Wilson offers fresh insight of this Christ-event with power and precision. She has married all-too-familiar lines of our carols with 31 Bible readings, rearticulating them in crisp profundity. Her poetry, honest of life's darkness and pain, complements her lively engagement. This book drives the reader to a new wonder of the pre-existent Son becoming 'Little Lord Jesus'. Reading this book will have you belting out carols with renewed vim and adoration for Emmanuel!

Natalie Brand
Author of several books, including *Prone to Wander: Grace for the Lukewarm and Apathetic*, and *The Good Portion – Salvation: The Doctrine of Salvation, for Every Woman*

Interweaving the wisdom and grace of her aptly termed Carolsville with the wonderous story of Jesus, Philippa Wilson in *Brightest and Best* sparks longing and love within us during the Advent and Christmas seasons. She welcomes us to share her deep love of the 'little Lord Jesus' – a mind-bending notion of the God who became Man. I commend it with joy.

Amy Boucher Pye
Author, *Celebrating Christmas*

What a delight this devotional work is! *Brightest and Best* is teeming with entry after entry of encouraging and convicting words that moved me to tears at times and caused me to simply rejoice at others. Deeply theological yet succinct and engaging, Philippa's work will serve to give readers a daily dose of significant insights into the wonder of our glorious Savior. We are drawn to greater affection for Christmas carols as Philippa skillfully selects poignant and sometimes neglected phrases from each one to give us new ways to praise our matchless Father for sending His Son to save us. I will definitely plan to read this book each December, although it is a treasure trove of uplifting joy all year round.

Mary K. Mohler
Author, *Growing in Gratitude*
Director, Seminary Wives Institute, Southern Baptist
Theological Seminary, Louisville, Kentucky

Brightest
and Best

31 Advent Devotions on Jesus

Philippa Ruth Wilson

CHRISTIAN
FOCUS

Copyright © Philippa Ruth Wilson 2022

hardback ISBN 978-1-5271-0874-5
ebook ISBN 978-1-5271-0925-4

10 9 8 7 6 5 4 3 2 1

Published in 2022
by
Christian Focus Publications, Ltd.
Geanies House, Fearn,
Ross-shire, IV20 1TW, Scotland.
www.christianfocus.com

Cover design by Daniel Van Straaten

Artwork (cover illustration and internals) by Rebekah Lesan

The Fell Types are digitally reproduced by
Igino Marini. www.iginomarini.com

Printed and bound by Gutenberg, Malta

CONTENTS

With gratitude to God for the life of Charles Wesley,
whose words have stirred thousands of tongues to sing
his great Redeemer's praise.

Hail, the heaven born Prince of Peace!
Hail the Sun of Righteousness;
Light and Life to all He brings,
Risen with Healing in His wings.

INTRODUCTION

'TIS THE SEASON

I cannot think of a better time for advent than at the end of November. I was born on December 1st, so my disdain for the month of November evidently began in the womb. To me, November seems to be an appropriate metaphor for the harshest parts of life in this world: it's cold, it's dark, and by the time it comes, I am utterly weary. Often, I stagger to the end of the month (or am blown there, by bitter winds that care nothing for my umbrellas or my dignity) and I feel utterly desperate for Christmas.

But perhaps, like me, as you hurtle towards the season 'to be jolly', it feels like mourning is more appropriate. In a world of poverty, prejudice, and pandemics, it's hard to sing ''tis the season to be jolly falalalalalalala!' and mean it (whatever falalalalalalala means?!). We are in a world laden with darkness and grief, and yet, by the end of November, so much around us seems to be yelling: HAVE A HAPPY CHRISTMAS! Is this what advent is then? A building pressure to put reality on hold for a while, and to just Have a Good Time?!

Thankfully, Isaiah cries out something different:

Comfort, comfort my people, says your God.
Speak tenderly to Jerusalem and cry out to her,
That her time of warfare has been fulfilled,
That the punishment of her iniquity has been pardoned,
That she has received from the LORD'S *hand double for all her*
sins. (Isa. 40:1, 2)

To people walking in the reality of the world as it is, in exhaustion, despair and mourning, God speaks tenderly. He's talking to people who deserve punishment, exile, alienation. But what He says to them, full of love, is: 'Comfort!' And what's the comfort?

In the wilderness prepare the way of the LORD; *make straight*
in the desert a highway for our God…. (Isa. 40:3)

The comfort of advent is that the Lord has come. It's the comfort that the Lord is coming. He has come! He is on the way! He Himself will be our comfort! Advent isn't the season to be 'jolly', so much as it is the season to be comforted. It's the season to remember that Jesus turned up, right when it was most dark and dry, where things were most broken and barren, and spoke, with every inch of His infinite being: comfort, comfort, comfort.

That is what this devotion is for. It's my hope that, as you read about the first coming of Jesus, and long for His second, you will know His comfort as you wait. Part One is focused on Christmas, and all that it means that Jesus has come. Part Two covers those days leading up to the new year; readings to cover that tricky post-Christmas period, to give you courage for whatever lies ahead. The best part of each devotion is the suggested Bible reading at the start; it won't take more than a few minutes to read the verses, but they will enrich each day beyond measure!

I hope that you have a truly happy season! Maybe even so happy you find out what falalalalalalalala means. But if you don't quite, or don't at all, may you encounter Jesus all the same. 'Tis the season to be … comforted, whether we are feeling jolly or not.

At the end of Revelation, Jesus says to the church, 'I am the bright and morning star' (Rev. 22:16) and it's those words that were the inspiration for the title of this book, words that come from a carol. I think they are beautiful adjectives for describing Jesus: He is the brightest and best, brighter and better than any star! As you read, I pray you will know Jesus: our hope, our consolation, our bright morning star.

PART 1

PREPARING FOR CHRISTMAS

DAY 1: EARTH STOOD HARD AS IRON

JESUS: SPRING IN OUR WINTER

Read: Ephesians 2:1-10

I f I had a penny for every time my former self rolled her eyes at poor Christina Rossetti over this carol, I would be able to make a lifetime's supply of figgy pudding. 'Oh, snow had fallen snow on snow, had it?' I'd cry, 'Yuletide in Bethlehem, was it!? Frosty wind made moan, did it? Mary and Joseph warmed themselves with pumpkin lattes, did they?!' I think a little differently now.

Just to be clear, I don't think Mary and Joseph were middle-class Westerners on the way to a frosty scene in Bethlehem, Yorkshire. But my older self is willing to give Tina the benefit of the doubt. Maybe it's because I like to consider her a writer pal, but I am willing to allow for the possibility that she is writing in metaphor. I've heard that writers enjoy that kind of thing.

When Isaiah says, 'And they will look to the earth, but behold, distress and darkness, the gloom of anguish. And they will be thrust into thick darkness' (Isa. 8:22), he's speaking metaphorically. The land of Judah is not prone to bouts of thick darkness any more than it is inclined to lie beneath eighteen layers of snow, but both metaphors are ways of describing the state of things before Jesus arrives.

I love Rossetti's imagery because it reminds me that Jesus came to a world that was hard and cold and impenetrable, and bleak and bleak and bleak. But in the same way He brought light to darkness, He brought warmth to coldness. It reminds me that, even now, He comes to situations and lives and hearts that are as hard as iron, and that His eyes are like flames of fire that melt and refine and warm and revive.

And it reminds me of the work He did in my heart. I had heard the gospel several hundred times before I *heard* the gospel. My heart stood hard as iron; my spirit was like a stone. I wanted to love God but didn't – and couldn't. In Paul's words, I was dead in my sin. In Wesley's words, 'Long my imprisoned spirit lay.' In Rossetti's words, 'Snow had fallen – snow on snow, snow on snow.'

I was buried in winter. And it was nothing in me that brought about spring. God made His light shine in my spirit and made His sun rise in my mind and the flames of joy blaze in a heart that had been solid ice.

I had grown up in a Christian home and had gone to church and to youth groups and even read my Bible (angrily) – but none of that made it click. God still felt distant, unknowable; my heart still felt cold, dead. Why was it the 100th time I heard the gospel that I loved it, clung to it, heard Jesus calling my name in it? Why not the 1st, or the 99th, or the 555th!? I don't know – but I know that one time, in the bleak midwinter, the sun came up. And it wasn't my doing. I'd sooner be able to dig myself out from under eighteen layers of snow. I was dead in my sin, but God made me alive with Christ. God did it!

This is what Rosetti celebrates: in the bleak midwinter, where we are powerless, helpless, desperate, and dead, Jesus comes. God does it!

> *The people who walked in darkness have seen a great light; those who dwelt in a land of deep darkness, on them light has shined. (Isa. 9:2)*

Jesus, Spring in our Winter: as You have before, once again, bring new life where there's death, beauty where there is brokenness, and warmth to our cold hearts.

DAY 2: FAR AS THE CURSE IS FOUND

JESUS: THE GARDENER

Read: Psalm 24

No more let sins and sorrows grow,
Nor thorns infest the ground;
He comes to make His blessings flow
Far as the curse is found.

The birth of Jesus isn't only a story about a remarkable man who grew up and saved his people. It is that. But at Christmas, Christians celebrate something far more all-encompassing. Christmas is a celebration that when Jesus was born, a redeemer was born. The Lord of glory entered a world burdened by a curse so He could redeem it. All of it!

The first man, Adam, made choices that brought a curse: his sin led to death and suffering and conflict. Every human since has made choices that have brought the same: destruction, frustration, isolation, toil, brokenness. All of nature groans under the brutal rule of a humanity whose kingdom is a kingdom of death.

But Jesus is born as the new first man: He is born of a woman to redeem those born of women, and to redeem creation that yearns for a better gardener to tend it! Jesus' birth bears witness: so far, humanity has failed. But it also says: there is new hope! God with us. God born a man. God of God, God's Son: Jesus.

Joyfully, Jesus gets being human right: from His first cry to His last – on a Roman cross – He loves, relies on, and lives for the glory of the God of heaven, just as humanity was made to do. Jesus brings blessing to the world, instead of a curse. Jesus is humanity who can ascend the hill of the Lord, with clean hands and a pure heart, the King of glory, mighty in the battle for righteousness from beginning to end.

He started to redeem humanity when He became humanity: He entered the world He had founded, He embodied what it is to be truly human, and then absorbed the curse to redeem us. Now, He sits at the right hand of the Father: the Son of Man, the Son of God, the Righteous One. He is the Redeemer: He has redeemed humanity, He has redeemed the curse and He is making all things new.

So, whatever seeming irredeemables we are currently facing in our lives, whatever the impenetrable knots of thistles and thorns may be, whatever the crushing millstones of oppression and captivity may be, whatever seems most tightly shrouded in unbreakable darkness – that is where the Redeemer has set His sights. He comes to make His blessings flow. Where? As far as the curse is found.

Christ redeemed us from the curse of the law by becoming a curse for us – for it is written: 'Cursed is anyone who is hanged on a tree' – so that the blessing of Abraham might come to the Gentiles… (Gal. 3:13, 14)

Lord Jesus, thank You that there is no part of creation that You will not redeem, no ground too hard for You to bring a harvest from it, no thistles too entangled for You to weed out and replace with beautiful blossom, no seed that has been buried that won't bloom. Help us believe it. Amen.

DAY 3: LET NOTHING YOU DISMAY!

JESUS: SON OF JOSEPH

Read: Matthew 1

When we meet Joseph, part-way through the first chapter of the New Testament, he cannot be having a good time. He has just found out that the woman he promised to marry is pregnant, and that the child is not his. He evidently cares deeply for Mary, because he doesn't want to disgrace her with a big, messy divorce, but, painful as it may be, ending the engagement seems essential.

If anyone is dismayed, surely it's Joseph, searching for a dignified way forward amid weighty disappointment and distress.

When the angel of the Lord appears to him in a dream, the first words spoken are, 'Joseph, son of David.' God speaks to Joseph in his dismay, and says, 'I know who you are.' By this point in Matthew, the reader knows who Joseph is! We've seen that the legal line of Jesus is traced through Joseph, through lines of glory and of suffering; we've seen the shame and the honor in it; we've seen that Jesus will be the son of Abraham, and the son of David. We may have read the genealogy and feel the writer's excitement, but Joseph hasn't.

But the angel of the Lord says, 'Joseph, son of David.' He reminds Joseph that there is more than what he sees right now. He is a descendent of Israel's greatest King, part of the family line that the promised Messiah would come from. Joseph may be a poor carpenter in some backwater, but he is also in the royal line.

The Lord tells Joseph that Mary's child is conceived of the Holy Spirit, that He will be called Immanuel and named Jesus. I love that Joseph isn't just told 'take Mary as your wife', but he is reassured, 'do not be afraid to take Mary as your wife.' Because of course he was afraid!

It's hard to imagine how hard it would have been for Joseph to obey this command. How much cynicism and mockery he might have faced for staying with Mary, how many times he might have had disgrace hurled at him. But here, the Lord speaks comfort to Joseph, and it gives him courage. When the time comes, Joseph 'called his name Jesus.' This sentence is massive; it's Joseph adopting Jesus as his own, giving Him the legal right to the throne of David, and naming Him with the name that declares belief in God's promise: He will save His people from their sins.

Although my life is so different to Joseph's, I'm so thankful that I worship the same Lord, who speaks comfort to us in times we are dismayed. The Lord, who reminds us of who we are, who says, 'don't be afraid to obey,' who gives us courage to walk on by faith and not by sight, because there is so much more to our situations than we see just now.

We look not to the things that are seen but to the things that are unseen. For the things that are seen are transient, but the things that are unseen are eternal. (2 Cor. 4:18)

Father God, please speak to us with words of comfort that will give us courage, so that we too might live not by sight, but by faith in Jesus, who saved His people from their sins. Amen.

DAY 4: MARY'S BOY CHILD

JESUS: SON OF MARY

Read: Luke 1:26-56

Often the focus of Mary's story is its extraordinary nature. This is more than understandable: a virgin birth is bound to be headline news! She's going to give birth to the Son of the Most High, and the baby will be conceived by the Holy Spirit. It is mysterious and baffling and, for some, even a stumbling block to belief. But Mary believes that the God who created the cosmos from nothing can create life in her womb – and she trusts Him.

What strikes me about this event is not so much how extraordinary it was, but how ordinary it was. Mary, like no one else, learnt that God works in the quiet, in the mundane, in the day-to-day. The angel came to her, not in a temple or a palace, but in lowly Nazareth.

And although the Messiah grows in her womb, Mary still must travel 100 miles to Bethlehem for a census, just like everyone else. The Son of the Most High depends on her for life, but it's not magical: it still involves being subject to the will of distant politicians and to long, inconvenient journeys and to closed doors and to the pain of childbirth and to the anxieties and confusions and exhaustions of motherhood.

But Mary understood that the coming of Jesus demonstrated God's commitment to the insignificant: 'He has exalted those of humble estate!' (v. 52) Mary shows us that God is at work in the ordinary. He does extraordinary, supernatural, and glorious deeds; He sends His own Son. But His son comes to us in the quiet. He comes to us in the regular humdrum of everyday life: in our traffic jams and our running out of milk and our thoroughly average office jobs, and there – where we are – He does incredible things.

Mary had to absorb an awful lot of mystery as she mothered Jesus. Luke says, 'Mary treasured up all these things, pondering them in her heart.' (Luke 2:19) She must have frequently felt perplexed by what the angel had promised when she saw her son's life unfold: from the manger and the shepherds, to His having to flee to Egypt, to the promised Messiah being a carpenter, to His brutal death on a Roman cross. Perhaps she expected something more impressive. I wonder whether her heart ever ached with the mystery: He's God's Son – why must it be this way? I know my heart has.

But I'm comforted when I remember that Mary was at the tomb on Easter Sunday. On that morning, when she saw her son, risen from the dead, how many of those treasured-up mysteries must have made sense. How her heart must have leaped and danced with delight at God's capacity to do good beyond her own understanding, beyond all those confusing days of Jesus' childhood. How those perplexities she'd stored up throughout His lifetime must have ignited and exploded like fireworks as her risen son explained them to her, their now significance revealed in the light of His life, and death, and risen life.

Mary reminds me that God is at work even when it looks unimpressive, and that He is at work even when I can't quite figure out how. All I can do is treasure up the mystery, and excitedly await the day when I meet the resurrected Son, and see His glorious work in all things revealed.

> *...for he has looked on the humble estate of his servant... from now on all generations will call me blessed. (Luke 1:48)*

Father God, thank You that You have come to the ordinariness of our lives, and that You are at work, even when it sometimes seems unimpressive. Help me to trust that You are at work amid all the mundane elements of my life, just as You were in Mary's. Amen.

DAY 5: FAITHFUL, JOYFUL AND TRIUMPHANT

JESUS: COUSIN OF JOHN

Read: Luke 1:5-25; 39-45

Dear Elizabeth,

I wanted to write to thank you for your faithful, joyful, triumphant life.

You were faithful. Luke writes about how you and Zechariah were righteous before God, walking blamelessly in all the statutes of the law. You weren't perfect – but you were faithful. Life for you hadn't turned out as you had hoped it would, yet you were faithful. You suffered the sadness and shame of never having had a child; there were some blessings you wanted but hadn't received, yet you still looked to the Lord and trusted Him. Later, when everyone expected your unexpected child to be named after Zechariah, you stayed faithful to what your husband had been told: 'No; he shall be called John.' You stood up for what was right, even when you were the only one who could. If I can have a little of your faithfulness in my life, I will be grateful.

You were also joyful. You delighted to support Mary as she carried Jesus in her womb. You were filled with the

Spirit and were able to say to your cousin: 'Blessed are you among women and blessed is the fruit of your womb!' (v. 42) If I had been in your situation, I might have felt envious of Mary – enjoying the benefits of childbirth in her youth, but more than that, bearing a son you knew would grow up to be greater than yours. But your joy was so abundant that it overflowed to bless Mary too. You were able to delight in her blessing, keeping your eyes fixed on the graciousness of God: 'Why is this granted to me that the mother of my Lord should come to me?' You encouraged her: keep believing in God's promise to you. Mary bubbled up in praise, and you paved the way for it. I know, in my life, I can be envious, and fixate on what I am lacking until I miss out on all the goodness God has given me. I'm inspired by your generosity to Mary. It's made me pray that I will have your gratitude and generosity of spirit in my life and relationships.

I wonder how much of your son's ministry you lived for? Did your heart swell with pride as he stood in the wilderness and cried, 'Behold the Lamb'? Did your heart break as John was put into prison, when Jesus said, 'The one who is least in the kingdom of heaven is greater than he'? (Matt. 11:11) Did you live to see him die for his faithfulness to the God you taught him to love? I bet you did not feel triumphant then.

But you raised a son who prepared the way for Jesus and modelled the path of following Him. He 'preached Him to all and cried in death: behold the Lamb!' In the same way that you, his mother, looked away from yourself to another – so did your son. He decreased so that Jesus might increase.

He was not the light, but he bore witness to the light. And in the only way that matters, he was triumphant. He lived and died proclaiming the One whose love was better than life, and whose life was stronger than death. Your son was like you, and I hope that in the days I have left before we hang out in glory, I might be able to be like him in his selfless, sensible commitment to Jesus, in his faithful, joyful witness to him. It makes my heart happy to know that even now, you are both living in the triumph of your choices to put your all in with Him.

Elizabeth, thank you for being such a model of faithful, joyful, triumphant faith. I can't wait to see you soon.

Blessed is she who believed there would be a fulfillment of what was spoken to her from the Lord! (Luke 1:45)

Father God, give us the faithful, joyful, suffering-now-triumph-later faith of Elizabeth, and the no-nonsense, Christ-honoring zeal of her son. For the glory of the Lamb of God, Amen.

DAY 6: O LITTLE TOWN OF BETHLEHEM

JESUS: SON OF DAVID

Read: The Book of Ruth

This poem tells the story of Ruth, the story of Bethlehem (which means, House of Bread, an appropriate birthplace for the Bread of Life!), and the story of how God ensured that Jesus, Son of David, would be born. The book of Ruth foreshadows the work and redemption of Jesus, and God's power to bring about good from grief, beauty from brokenness.

I wonder if Mary and Joseph thought about it on their road to the city of David. As they struggled to find a place to stay, I wonder if they remembered their great-great grandmother, who had also taken the road to Bethlehem, against all odds, with the faithfulness of the Father, her only hope.

We stood at their gravesides and wept—
grief shattered our hearts into a
thousand directions;
hope seeped out through the cracks
until our hearts were as dry as the land.

Dry as the ocean floor,
when hungry slaves walked home.
They said, 'There is bread in Bethlehem.'
So we took that road,
parched and emptied–
and though we cleaved to each other,
grief was a cleaver too. She left–

But I would die on the road to Bethlehem,
because a God who made a path of dust through waves
could surely birth an oasis in the desert.
And even if he didn't,
'How could he?' she said–
And even if he didn't,
I'd rather die under the wings of the God
who provides a ram,
the God of the nations,
than in the land of any other god.
So we wept, and I clung on, and we wept.

I died on the road to Bethlehem.

Yes, I died on the road to Bethlehem.
But seeds die in the ground,
and in the darkness of the soil,
give birth to mighty oaks,
to towering trees,
and to family trees.
There was bread in Bethlehem,
and the dead man's widow
brought home more seed than she could carry,
and became more blessed than seven sons.

We stood at the crib side and sang,
joy flooding our hearts and filling
the cracks of estuaries:
the redeemer had a son,
a servant,
and their seed – ours,
would be a Servant Redeemer,
a root that would grow in dry land,
and become an oasis in the desert;
the Lamb provided by God,
a refuge for the nations.

And Joseph also went up from Galilee, from the town of
Nazareth, to Judea, the city of David, which is called
Bethlehem, because he was of the house and lineage of David,
to be registered with Mary, his betrothed, who was with child.
(Luke 2:4,5)

Father God, thank You for Your faithfulness through the ages, and the story that tells of a coming redeemer who would bring blessing to the nations. Through us, today, would You extend the blessing of Christ to the nations again, even as we hope in Him. Amen.

DAY 7: COME, THOU DAYSPRING!

JESUS: THE BRIGHTEST DAWN

Read: Luke 1:67-80

O come, Thou Day-Spring, come and cheer
Our spirits by Thine advent here.
Disperse the gloomy clouds of night
And death's dark shadows put to flight!
Rejoice! Rejoice! Emmanuel
Shall come to thee, O Israel.

Because of the tender mercy of our God, whereby the sunrise
shall visit us from on high to give light to those who sit in
darkness and in the shadow of death, to guide our feet into the
way of peace. (Luke 1:78, 79)

It's darkest before sunrise.

The air is cold, heavy. Obscurity muffles sound; a shroud of silence. It seems impossible that morning could ever come.

Suddenly: a horizon.

Where there has been no division, a rapid glow expands to a flash skyline: the darker shades are pushed northwards in its defining, their disappearance made inevitable as the radiance intensifies. A thousand royal hues expand and rotate to herald the arrival of the sun.

A golden orb emerges: a fiery ball whose commanding ascent prompts the dawn chorus.

Its movement is swift: now it is not just the horizon that is defined. As the light explodes the composition of the landscape is brought into rich definition: countless textures, tones, nuances and glories are exposed by the generosity of its flare.

It is not long until its radiance cannot contain itself: clouds have fled; the gloom has been swallowed up.

The golden river gushes into every last crevice: shadows are chased away as the round gets higher.

All there is to see can be seen now: delicate petals and dewy cobwebs and shimmering leaves, valleys and contours and wave-crests, reflections in puddles and waterfall froth and pond ripples, broad avenues and swathes of forest and individual blades of grass in countless shades. The rays have awakened vibrancy, not just in an outbreak of every conceivable colour, but in movement and in sound: flowers open, ice melts, meadows glisten, and the morning is alive with the chatter of hopes, the laughter of play, the purposefulness of work.

There is life now.

Life in countless distinctions, shades and tinges; life that swells and responds and finds its source in the Light; life that comes from the sunrise.

The Light shines in the darkness, and the darkness has not overcome it. (John 1:5)

God of God, Light of Lights. Shine Your light into our darkness – bring life, and warmth, and hope. And help us to serve You with joy, all our days. Amen.

DAY 8: LO, HE ABHORS NOT THE VIRGIN'S WOMB

JESUS: OUR BROTHER

Read: Philippians 2:5-11

God of God, Light of Light;
Lo, he abhors not the Virgin's womb!
Very God, begotten not created!
O come let us adore him!

I have included the minimum amount of exclamation marks appropriate for this carol. The wonder of the incarnation is that Jesus, who is God, who is Light, who is not a created being, who is in every way God, does not regard Mary's womb with hatred or disgust. In the words of Wesley, He is 'pleased as man with man to dwell'! He takes the nature of a servant and for the joy set before Him is willing to submit to a womb, even though wombs were His idea in the first place!

So that He might be with us in our darkness, not only did He not reject the womb, but He also did not reject poverty, or danger, or becoming a refugee. He did not turn away from weakness; He did not turn away from rejection; He did not turn away from violence, humiliation, shame, even death: He did not abhor the womb, and He did not abhor the cross. He was obedient to birth and obedient to death: Christ the Lord was born to us, lived for us, and died for us. He was given in our place.

And Jesus delighted to do so.

He was willing to become flesh and make His dwelling among us. His becoming a servant was an act of joyful obedience to the Father: He wanted to come to redeem us; He wanted to take on our flesh; He wanted to save us from our sins. That's why Hebrews says for the 'joy that was set before him he endured the cross, despising the shame' (Heb. 12:2): He laid down His life, of His own accord, for my sake, for my joy.

There is plenty about myself that I feel ashamed of. Some of it justified, some not. But this carol reminds me, either way: He is not ashamed to call me His. He did not reject the Virgin's womb, because He would not reject me. He did what it took so that my redemption would be possible. He became obedient to death because my rescue, my reconciliation to the Father, my redeemed heart, my joy, would bring Him joy.

He is not ashamed to call us brothers and sisters! He is not ashamed to have become man for our sake! He is not ashamed to share in our flesh and our blood, and then to have it broken and poured out for our redemption. Because of His incredible grace and power and redemptive mercy, He is not ashamed of me.

O Come, let us adore Him! Christ, the Lord!

Since therefore the children share in flesh and blood, he himself likewise partook of the same things, so that through death he might destroy the one who has the power of death, that is, the devil. (Heb. 2:14)

Jesus, I cannot fathom Your humility, that though You were there before time began, You did not despise the womb, but took joy in entering it, so that I might enter Your glory. Fill me with wonder at Your worth today. Amen.

DAY 9: LITTLE LORD JESUS

JESUS: MANGER-MESSIAH
Read: Luke 2:1-7

'Away in the Manger' is not my favorite carol. I find it a little dull. But the line that riles me most is the classic, 'the cattle are lowing, the baby awakes, but little Lord Jesus, no crying he makes.' A hungry and human baby in a manger, surrounded by mooing, is probably going to cry, whatever moral lesson you are trying to teach Victorian children. I side with 'Once in Royal' on this one: 'tears and smiles like us he knew', and I'd wager Mary would too!

However, in its favour, this carol does contain a three-word theological bomb that blows every other idea humanity has ever had about God right out of the water: little Lord Jesus. 'Little Lord Jesus' is the wonder of the incarnation in three words. Yes, Charles Wesley wrote: 'Our God contracted to a span, incomprehensibly made man!' and, 'Hail th'incarnate deity!' so I could have used either of those for a title. But I love the audacity of these three simple words. Little. Lord. Jesus!

Jesus is God become little. He's born to a woman and, as such, born vulnerable and weak and hungry and utterly dependent on His young, confused, weary parents, who had nowhere to lay Him but in a feeding trough. Of course His tiny hands stretched out for comfort, of course His miniscule lungs cried out for food.

The birth of any baby is miraculous. Which parents can stand in the delivery room without some profound sense of wonder at the preciousness of a little human life? But the miracle of Jesus' birth is not just that He's little. He is the Lord.

In terms of his significance, Jesus is anything but little. He is the least little being in the universe – in terms of His worth and His glory and His might. He is the Lord! The one whose minute frame is wrapped in swaddling cloths is born into the world He created. The one by whom stars were flung into expansive galaxies, the one through whom DNA was penned in all its glorious intricacies and nuances, the one who assigned the sea its limit and crafted the mountain ranges on a thousand planets – this is the one lying on the straw. But He became little. Why?

Because His name is Jesus. 'Jesus' meaning: He will save His people from their sins. He shared in our humanity so that He might break the curse over our humanity. The One who has been majestic and glorious and mighty through all eternity became the little Lord Jesus, so that we might be rescued.

She will bear a son, and you shall call his name Jesus, for he will save his people from their sins. (Matt. 1:21)

Little, Lord Jesus. You created the heavens, and yet You became little so that you could save us. Fill us with wonder at Your humility, and Your majesty! And make us more like You. Amen.

DAY 10: GO, TELL IT ON THE MOUNTAIN

JESUS: GOOD NEWS FOR ALL

Read: Luke 2:8-20

The shepherds were not expecting the skies to be aflame with angels that night. I mean, who could have expected it? It was a truly remarkable night.

Made remarkable by all of those other unremarkable nights: days and weeks and months and years of nights where the skies were silent and their lives were small and unimpressive. They were poor in a culture where richness equated blessing, field-dwelling sheep herders in a culture that valued cleanliness, working nights in a culture that thrived in daytime.

So, when the angels announce good news of great joy for all the people, they start with the people whom the world would have expected to be furthest from it. The poor, the unclean, the outsiders.

I bring you good news of a great joy that will be for all the people. For unto you is born this day in the City of David a Saviour, who is Christ the Lord. And this will be a sign for

you: you will find a baby wrapped in swaddling cloths and
lying in a manger. (Luke 2:10-11)

The Messiah is born, the angel declares, and this is how
you'll know: He's lying in a food trough.

And then the whole sky is riven with angels singing about
the glories of God.

I cannot imagine the wonder of the shepherds as they
stammered to one another with heaven's crescendo still
ringing in their ears: 'Let's go to Bethlehem and see this thing
that has happened, which the Lord has told us about.'(v. 15)
Us!? In awe, they hurry off and find the baby in a manger.
The baby who is Israel's anointed King; the baby who is the
Lord. And they find that this precious baby, the Lord, is
in many ways, not unlike them: He is poor, He is hanging
out with unclean animals, He is lying in an animal's feeding
manger, because there was 'no place' for Him elsewhere.

This story reminds me that no one is excluded from joy.
When I am finding it most difficult to believe that happiness
is possible, I remember that the angel promised that Jesus
was a great joy for all people. The world says happiness is
possible for the wealthy and the attractive and healthy and
the career savvy and for the successful and for the loved and
for the included. But the angels say: Jesus is good news of
great joy for the shepherds, for all the people, for me.

After they've found the Manger-Messiah, the shepherds
return to the fields. Their circumstances have not changed,
but their perspective has. The King in the trough is their
King and as their hearts swell in wonder and glory, they

cannot help but to go tell it on the mountain: He is Heaven's joy – and He's for all the people.

> *And let the one who is thirsty come; let the one who desires take the water of life without price. (Rev. 22:17)*

Father God, thank You for Your gift of grace— Jesus Himself, the Manger-Messiah, is a gift for me too. Help me to receive Him today, with joy so like the shepherd's joy that I cannot keep it to myself. Amen.

DAY 11: HEAVENLY HOSTS SING, HALLELUJAH

JESUS: SONG OF THE ANGELS

Read: Luke 2:8-20

Suddenly there was with the angel a multitude of the heavenly host praising God and saying: 'Glory to God in the highest and on earth peace among those on whom his favor rests! (Luke 2:14)

I can't help but feel that this line does not belong in a carol called 'Silent Night.' When heaven's army-choir filled the skies to praise God for the wisdom and grace and power and beauty of the incarnation, as they praised Him for His peace and favor and kindness to humanity in need of a Saviour, the night was surely anything but silent.

What incredible sounds must have reverberated around the heavens as those who had beheld Jesus face to face from the beginning tried to sing His glories: what melodies, what harmonies, what a range of perfect notes, what a blend of unexpected harmonies must have sounded from this Choir of choirs. How it must have contrasted with the silent night!

I find it amazing to think that this is what accompanies the announcement of the Champion of Heaven being born in a manger. The angels do not accompany 'a Saviour has been born to you!' with a rebuke to the Shepherds: 'Look what you made God do.' Oh no, the angels sing of God's grace and delight in sending His Son. Apart from anything else, this heavenly chorus is a reminder that the Father was not reluctant to give His Son to be a Saviour. The heavenly host sing a song of triumph and celebration: peace, favour and glory, glory, glory to God. Glory to a God who is glad to send salvation! Glory to a God who is glad to be our Saviour! The angels sing in wonder: here is a Saviour who will go to the womb, to the manger, to a crown of thorns, to the cross, to the grave, to glory! Here is a Saviour who will throw another heavenly party every time a sinner hopes in Him!

Glory to God in the highest, indeed!

Praise the Lord! Praise the Lord from the heavens; praise him in the heights! Praise him, all his angels; praise him, all his hosts! (Ps. 148:1, 2)

Lord Jesus, You are the song of the angels. Be our song too! Would our hearts soar with the joy of knowing You did not leave us without rescue: You are our Saviour, born to us! Give us grace to sing out in joy, even amidst our pain. Amen.

DAY 12: REST BESIDE THE WEARY ROAD

JESUS: REST-GIVER

Read: Psalm 23

O ye beneath life's crushing load,
Whose forms are bending low,
Who toil along the climbing way
With painful steps and slow;
Look now, for glad and golden hours
Come swiftly on the wing;
Oh rest beside the weary road
And hear the angels sing.

Advent reminds us of where we are in the story: we're not at its end yet; we're still on the road.

Like Mary on the road to Bethlehem, we are plodding onwards, but we are heavy-laden and weary. Someone exciting is on the way, but, from where we are right now, His coming seems more distant than the stars. We are toiling. We are climbing. We are waiting. The way forward is arduous, perseverance is painful, and rewards seem few.

But the song of the angels is for those who are crushed beneath life's weight. It is those whose journeys feel unrelentingly long and inexpressibly frustrating and insurmountably steep who need to hear the golden song of the angels:

A Saviour is born to you who will be for all the people; he is Christ the Lord.

The song of the angels is also for those who are crushed beneath their own expectations. It is for those who are constantly striving for an unattainable perfection, whose Decembers are heavy with lists of things they must do and must do well, who have the law crying, 'Run!' and 'Do better!' and who feel compelled to, without the energy or capacity to do so. It is they who need to hear the glad song of the angels:

A Saviour is born to you who will be for all the people; he is Christ the Lord.

The coming Messiah will *'stand and shepherd his flock in the strength of the LORD, in the majesty of the LORD his God'* (Micah 5:4).

The coming of a shepherd is also a glorious command to rest. It is not the sheep but the shepherd who defends the flock, fights for the flock, leads the flock. The Good Shepherd meets the needs of His flock, so that the flock can lie down beside still waters.

Yes, the burden of life may feel overwhelming – for the suffering and for the striving. But the angel's song is for those who cannot stay above the waves, for those whose arms are weary from the struggle, for those whose strength is spent. The angels sing of the birth of a Saviour who is coming to lift the burden of His people, a Saviour who will carry it all the way to the cross.

Run, John, run! The law demands
and gives me neither feet nor hands.
Far better news the gospel brings,
It bids us fly and gives us wings.
(Attributed to John Bunyan)

Come to me all you who labor and are heavy laden, and I will give you rest. (Matt. 11:28)

Father God, whatever else happens this Christmas, would we give our burdens to Jesus, and receive His rest. For His glory, Amen.

DAY 13: BRIGHTER VISIONS BEAM AFAR

JESUS: WISDOM OF THE AGES

Read: Matthew 2:1-10

> *Wise men, leave your contemplations!*
> *brighter visions shine afar;*
> *seek in him the hope of nations,*
> *you have seen his rising star!*

Like many teenagers, I took a bus to get to school. I distinctly remember feeling that what made the journey was whether Red Dragon FM played Aerosmith ('I Don't Wanna Miss a Thing') en route. Another highlight of the trip was passing a church billboard with posters emblazoned on it in various shades of neon, rotating according to season. During the World Cup they had one that said: 'Stuck in a Corner? Go For the Cross!' and at Christmas they had that well-known proverb: 'Wise Men Sought Jesus; Wise Men Still Do.' As a fifteen-year-old new Christian, it seemed clear enough to me that I wasn't following Jesus because of my own wisdom. My own wisdom had declared God distant and my life joyless; His wisdom had called me by name and had given me hope and joy inexpressible: it was His mercy, rather than my wisdom, that led me to follow Him.

But I've since wondered about the Magi: were they wise? Yes, in that they had some degree of earthly knowledge: they could study vast stretches of stars and, from their scrutiny, learn of the birth of the King of the Jews. They had the insight to see the importance of this occasion, and they had common sense: they went to the palace. And perhaps the biggest yes is that they cared about the meaning of life! They were wise to seek out answers about what ultimately mattered, to use all they had in pursuit of them.

God is at work in all kinds of ways to make Himself known. There is value in using our reason and our wonder at creation and the historical record and intellectual rigour to seek Him; all these pursuits are gifts from the One who makes Himself known to those who seek Him; all are evidence of His mercy. But the wisdom of the Magi had its

limits. Their own wisdom led them to an insecure tyrant, rather than to Emmanuel.

It was the finding of Jesus, much more than the seeking of Him, that made them wise. As the star settled over the place where a little Jewish boy lived, weak and poor, they learnt true wisdom. As they fled the wrath of a despot who saw the Manger-Messiah as his enemy, they learnt a wisdom beyond fathoming and absolute, sheer folly in the eyes of the world. The Wisdom of God, the One through whom the heavens were established, embraced all that humanity considered most foolish: He embraced weakness and death. And, as the Magi worshipped the fragile, surprising, soon-to-be-refugee King of the Jews, their hearts must have been humbled, their understanding of life uprooted, and their own wisdom radically transformed. The inadequacy of their scholarship and intellect must have been revealed in light of the inexpressible glories of the unworldly wisdom of God.

When I think of the Magi worshipping Jesus, I am reminded of the limits of my own earthly wisdom. When I find it impossible to understand situations that just seem wretched in the world, in my own life, I am challenged to remember the Magi. They could read the stars but bowed low before the Wisdom of the manger. They recognized a greater wisdom, and remembering this helps me bow before God's wisdom, too.

Blessed is the one who finds wisdom. (Prov. 3:13a)

Father God, make us wise as we bow before Jesus, the Wisdom of God. Show us the limits of earthly wisdom, and the worth of the King in the manger, that we might be truly wise. Amen.

DAY 14: IN HIS NAME ALL OPPRESSION SHALL CEASE

JESUS: A BETTER KING

Read: Matthew 2:13-18

The Massacre of the Innocents is not one of the Christmas narratives the Western church tends to dwell on. These verses in Matthew are a horrific account of the brutal execution of thousands of innocent children.

When Herod learns that the Magi are looking for a new-born King, he is alarmed by this potential threat to his power: he is determined to control the situation and protect himself. He tells the men searching for Jesus to let him know where they have found Him so that he 'too may come and worship him,' but, when it becomes clear that control has slipped beyond his grasp and the Magi will not return, he is more outraged than ever.

In a typically futile, typically dictatorial attempt to secure his own supremacy, the paranoid ruler orders that every Bethlehem boy under the age of two be slaughtered. And they are. Thousands of innocent children suffer under one person's ruthless desire to stay in control. As a result, there is weeping and loud lamentation and no place for comfort.

It's tempting to write this off as an obscure event from antiquity. But children across the globe, today, in Afghanistan, in Myanmar, in Yemen, suffer similar atrocities: victims of decisions made by power-grabbing adults in worlds far removed from their little spheres. War marches into child-sized lives and brings with it displacement, violence, hunger. The Massacre of the Innocents is not an event from antiquity, but a fitting title for much of our own era.

Perhaps it is tempting to see the Massacre as being something relevant then to other places: insane, and evil, but nothing to do with me in my calm, measured, bloodshed-free life.

Recently I've realized that I don't have much of a leg to stand on in my scorn of Herod. I have a similar reckless determination to rule my own life and protect my own reputation in a way that shows no regard for how it might make the undeserving suffer. I, too, have railed violently against the threat of another king, come to reign over my world and life and choices.

So often, when I want to be king in my own life, it is those who least deserve it who suffer most at my temper and my selfishness. Not least, the boy in the manger.

In Bethlehem, the baby escaped an execution at the hands of sinful men – for the time being. He did not escape being an innocent sufferer. A few decades later, He faced execution, again. And the King of the Jews suffered, and then died, because of the countless 'wannabe' kings desperate to terminate His rightful rule. I am not Herod.

But I am responsible for the suffering of an Innocent. I am not Herod. But I am also not a good king.

Like Herod, my rule of my own life results in anguish and weeping and mourning that cannot be comforted.

But into the manger is born a King, in whose name all oppression shall cease. He is a King who surrenders His power, who serves the weak, who brings comfort to the mourning, who will grow up and shepherd His people until He lays down His life for them.

Of the increase of his government and peace there will be no end, on the throne of David and over his kingdom, to establish it and uphold it with justice and with righteousness from this time forth and forevermore. (Isa. 9:7)

Father God, what glorious news that Jesus is King! Please bring justice and peace to those who suffer across the world, and please use me, as I submit to the rule of Jesus, to serve those causes too. Amen.

DAY 15: LET EARTH RECEIVE HER KING

JESUS: THE BEST KING

Read: John 13:1-20

So, Jesus is not like Herod. Or me. Alleluia!

'Joy to the World' is one of my favorite carols because it so simply states what Christmas is all about: joy. Despite everything our sinful nature tells us, the coming of this King, who surpasses us in authority and power and significance, is indescribably good news. His coming in history and His coming in the future are both events that give us immeasurable cause to celebrate.

Because I like to be king in my life, the sound of a coming king can sound – as it did to Herod – like a threat. But this carol joyfully advises, 'Let earth receive her King!' Receive your King! His rule will be a good idea!

But how do we know? What is this King like?

Jesus, knowing that the Father had given all things into his hands, and that he had come from God and was going back to God, rose from supper. He laid aside his outer garments, and taking a towel tied it around his waist. Then he poured water into a basin and began to wash the disciples' feet and to wipe them with the towel that was wrapped around him. (John 13:3-5)

Then Jesus called the disciples to him and said, 'I have compassion on the crowd because they have been with me now three days and have nothing to eat. And I am unwilling to send them away hungry, lest they faint on the way. (Matt. 15:32)

And when they came to the place that is called the Skull, there they crucified him… and Jesus said, 'Father, forgive them, for they know not what they do.' (Luke 23:33, 34)

Let Earth receive her King!

Here is a King who uses His power to serve His people; a King of compassion, of mercy; a King whose coronation is with a crown of thorns; who pleads forgiveness for His executors; whose wisdom silences His enemies; whose generosity provides more than a thousand bottles of wine for shamed wedding planners; whose wit comes up with such imagery as 'you strain out a gnat to swallow a camel'; who looks after bruised reeds and who makes breakfast on the beach for those who abandoned Him in His darkest hour. Why would we want another king?!

This King coming is a reason for joy! He is a better King than there has ever been – and He is certainly a better King than me! This is a King whose coming gives us reason to sing and celebrate and delight and hope.

Blessed is he who comes in the name of the Lord! (Ps. 118:26)

Lord Jesus, we are so thankful You came as King, and we look forward to You coming again! Give us grace to accept You as King – today, and every day of our lives, so that we might have great joy and You might get great glory. Amen.

DAY 16: WORD OF THE FATHER, NOW IN FLESH APPEARING!

JESUS: GOD MADE MAN

Read: John 1:1-14

A few years ago on Twitter, famous comedian John Cleese let loose on the world of 'evangelicals', complaining that Christians continue to follow the God of the Old Testament when Jesus is so evidently different to Him. He asked, 'Why would you need to be God-fearing if Jesus is your God?' And that was a tell-tale sign he might not have read the New Testament recently.

The New Testament is full of people who are afraid of Jesus. There is something terrifying about someone who has power over demons, and over the weather, who can outwit you with His wisdom, who can gain the approval of people but who doesn't pursue it, who can radically transform someone beyond recognition, who won't back down from religious rulers, from Pilate, from Herod. People who meet Jesus in the New Testament are afraid of Him.

If you like Jesus because you don't think you have anything to fear, then whoever it is you like, it isn't Jesus. As

the much-quoted line from Narnia goes, when Lucy asks if Aslan is safe:

> *'Safe?' said Mr. Beaver; 'Who said anything about safe? 'Course he isn't safe. But he's good. He's the King, I tell you.'* [1]

What makes the God of the Bible, both and Old and New Testaments, terrifying is not His badness, but His perfect goodness. His unrelenting holy, holy, holiness is enough to make the best of humanity quake in their sinful boots.

But Cleese did raise a concern that many people have. They think – *okay, I could have Jesus as my King, but I'm not sure about the God He comes to represent.* But the King we considered yesterday is God's truest expression of Himself.

1   Lewis, C S, and Pauline Baynes. *The Lion, the Witch, and the Wardrobe* (New York, NY: HarperTrophy, 1994).

One of the most fundamental tenets of Biblical faith is the belief that, in Christ, the fullness of God lives in bodily form. And yet, it is so tempting to buy the popularly-held belief that God is harsh and erratic and capricious and ruthless, while Jesus is the apologetic Son who turns up and says something like, 'Honestly he's not that bad once you get to know him.' Nonsense.

Jesus turns up and says, 'Whoever has seen me has seen the Father' (John 14:9). Jesus is the Word of God. He perfectly communicates what His Father is like. He is not a PR representative sent to compensate or to paper over all the cracks of how God the Father's reputation has been sullied. No, He comes to express the nature of the Father with absolute accuracy. When we see Jesus, we see an intense highlight reel of all the Father is and has been for all of eternity. When we see Jesus' compassionate tenderness, miraculous power, staggering mercy, care for the outcasts, attentiveness to children, inclusion of women, restoration of rejects, healing of the diseased, rebuking of the religious, we see the Father.

For in [Christ] all the fullness of God was pleased to dwell. (Col. 1:19)

Father God, thank You that in seeing Jesus, we see You. You are like Jesus! You are kind, and merciful, and not safe, but full of love. Help us to see You as You are, in Jesus. Amen

DAY 17: THE HOPES AND FEARS OF ALL THE YEARS

JESUS: THE SALVATION OF GOD

Read: Luke 2:25-35

The hopes and fears of all the years are met in Thee tonight.

This passage is extraordinary. Simeon is a devout man who has been waiting for the 'consolation of Israel.' He's aware of the hardness of life and the lostness of his nation. On this day, he comes into the temple, and, when Jesus is brought in, he declares to God: 'My eyes have seen your salvation!' Simeon isn't holding a set of laws in his hands. He's not holding the Ten Commandments, or a to-do list, or a doctrine, or a manifesto, or a philosophy or a state of soul. He's holding Jesus.

He's holding Jesus and he's saying to the Lord: 'My eyes have seen Your salvation!' The good news of Christmas is not that God has given us a very specific, very demanding set of laws we ought to complete to be good enough to make it on to His cosmic 'Nice List.' Hallelujah, God is not like Santa Claus.

Simeon can hold the salvation of God in his arms and say: this is the way Israel will be comforted; this is the way the nations will see the reality of who God is; this is the way the thoughts of many hearts will be revealed. The salvation of God is Jesus. He is a person. He is a person whose life, even as He is in the temple being presented to the Lord, will bring righteousness to many. The consolation of Israel, the consolation of the nations, is Jesus.

The solution to our sadness, sin, and suffering is not a doctrine, or a to-do list, or a philosophy or a state of mind because each of these things – and all of them together – are patently inadequate for the problems they aim to solve. The solution to our sadness, sin, and suffering is not simple, because these things are not simple. But this does not mean there is not a solution.

Simeon held Jesus in his arms and saw the salvation of God: a person. And not just a person, but the Ultimate Person. Not just a bringer of peace, but the Prince of Peace. And not just complex, but an 'admirable conjunction of diverse excellencies' (Jonathan Edwards). He is the Lion, and the Lamb. He is the Treasure of Heaven, who for our sake became poor. He is the Creator of Life who laid down His life. He is the humble King born in a manger, who grew up to declare boldly: 'I am the way, the truth, and the life. No one comes to the Father except through me.' (John 14:6)

He is the salvation of the Lord.

For the Lord God is my strength and song, and He has become my salvation. (Isa. 12:2)

Lord Jesus, You are our salvation! Thank You so much that You are a person: the most glorious, complex person, sufficient for all the ways we need rescuing. Be our strength and our song today, as we thank You for Your salvation. Amen.

DAY 18: EMMANUEL SHALL COME TO THEE

JESUS: GOD WITH US

Read: Luke 2:36-38

Anna was an eighty-four-year-old woman who, following the death of her husband after only seven years of marriage, had moved to the temple. She had decided: I will make God's presence my home. She had lost out on the chance of her own household, and so she went to the temple, God's dwelling, and set up home there. In her loss, she said to God: I will be with you. She made Him her hope, her refuge and her home. This act of faith showed that Anna knew something of the generous grace of God, as one who provides for widows and comforts the broken hearted. But I love to imagine how her heart must have leapt when she heard Simeon declare: 'Here is the salvation of the Lord!'

She had known the grace of God that welcomed her when she said, 'I will be with you.' But she'd now met Emmanuel, the God who left the glories of heaven and said to His people: '*I* will be with *you*.' From His fullness we have all received grace in the place of grace!

Years earlier, King David had said to God: I will build you a house! And God had replied: No, I will build you a house. God outgave David, in generosity beyond fathoming. In fact, the child in Simeon's arms was the fulfillment of that very promise: here was the one who would reign on David's throne forever, the one whose government and peace would increase into eternity. And here was Anna, the humble widow, being outgiven by the same God, through the same child.

For God to say, 'You can be with me' is generous and miraculous and glorious beyond our fathoming. But what He actually says (and then does!) is more generous than that: 'I will be with you.' And when God promises, 'I will be with you', He doesn't just mean He will be where we are. He means, I will be your representative; I will fight the battle for you; I will unite you to me; I will dwell in your heart; I will be your refuge; I will make your heart my home.

However generous we think God is, He is more generous than that. We may say to God, 'I will be where You are', though we don't have the power to bridge the enormous divide between us. But God says to us, 'I will be with you.' And then He bridges that gap between us until our lives are hidden with Christ in God.

Be content with what you have, for he has said, 'I will never leave you nor forsake you.' (Heb. 13:5)

Thank You, God of grace, for sending Jesus to be with us. Thank You that He will never leave us or forsake us. Give us eyes to see Your grace and generosity today and show us how we can pass it on. In the name of Emmanuel, Amen.

DAY 19: OUR WEAKNESS IS NO STRANGER

JESUS: MAN OF SORROWS

Read: Isaiah 53

He is familiar with grief.
That sledge-hammer slam of loss, of shock – He's stood
beneath its blow.
He knows what it is to mourn,
to feel the sting of death,
to weep – face to face with its concrete full-stop blockading
hope for future goodness.
He is acquainted with the stench of decay,
He's cried tears of desperation.

He is familiar with pain.
With wounds, with aches, with the most destructive of disease
– He's buckled, He's been brought low.
He knows what it is to be weak,
to bear sorrows and to stumble;
to bleed
in a broken flesh, gaining scars that time won't heal.
He is acquainted with the stripes and the shame,

He's pled for another way.

He is familiar with rejection,
With standing shelterless in the storm.
He's been exposed; alone.
He's seen friendship without faithfulness,
family without home:
forsaken,
faces He loved turning away, one by one by One.
He is acquainted with nights of longing,
He's known dark and silent skies.

He knows our need; our weakness is no stranger.

He is familiar with waiting,
bearing the burden of precious promises,
He's known their fulfilment seeming slow.
He's had no hope but God,
no life but in resurrection.
Entombed.

He's relied upon on a Love stronger than death,

and He has been vindicated.
By a Power stronger than the grave,
He has been led through the darkest valley,
and brought to a victory feast.

He is acquainted with glory,
He's known darkness turned to light—

Weeping turned to joy.
He's ascended, with great power – and He leads captives in
His train.

For if we have been united with him in a death like his, we
shall certainly be united with him in a resurrection like his.
(Rom. 6:5)

Then we who are alive, who are left, will be caught up together
with them in the clouds to meet the Lord in the air, and so we
will always be with the Lord. (1 Thess. 4:17)

Father God, thank You for Jesus – the God who knows what it is to suffer, what it is to be brought low, what it is to have His body broken. Because of this, because of Him, help us to trust You. Amen.

DAY 20: HE SHARETH IN OUR GLADNESS

JESUS: JOY-SHARER

Read: Isaiah 9:1-7

Not only is Jesus acquainted with our sorrows, but He shares in our happiness too. Our gladness matters to the Creator of the Universe! This is a beautiful thing to remember during a season that can be rich with good gifts.

Every good thing, Christmassy or not, is a gift from Him, given for our delight and joy. Frosty mornings and warming hot chocolates and the smell of pine needles and the warmth of log fires and prettily flickering candles and the cutest of nativity plays and the swell of a choir in full song and the goodness of mulled wine and mince pies and Terry's Chocolate Orange and countless other blessings, in this and every season, are given to make our hearts glad. We were made to have hearts that are brim-full, overflowing with gratitude to the Great Giver of all these things!

So often though, my heart is hard and shrivelled, rather than glad. In fact, without the cross, each of these gifts would stand only as reminders of my lack of gratitude towards

God, that though I have known His goodness, I have not acknowledged Him or given Him thanks.

But the story of Christmas is a story of a God who is zealously committed to my joy: Jesus came to share the gladness of God with me. From all eternity, Jesus has been the Beloved of God, and through His life and death and resurrection, Jesus has shared His belovedness with us. He's made a way for us to know God and, in knowing Him, to find great joy! In Isaiah 53:12, it says that after the Suffering Servant has seen the light of life, 'he will divide the spoils with the many.' Jesus is depicted as a mighty warrior who returns from a brutal battle as victor, carrying the bounty of His victory in his scarred hands. And Jesus, wonderful Saviour that He is, intends for us to share His spoils.

Have you ever read Zephaniah 3 and doubted that it could be about you? In it, the Lord says to Zion: 'he will rejoice over you with gladness; he will quiet you by his love; he will exult over you with loud singing.' (Zeph. 3:17) If I struggle to imagine God singing with such delight over me, I imagine Him whooping and rejoicing and belting out a song of joy over Jesus, who, though He was in very nature God made Himself nothing, so that His Father would be glorified, and His people would be redeemed. Of course, I can imagine that! The Father is absolutely enthralled with Jesus!

And that's the delight, the joy, 'the spoils' Jesus invites us to share in; the gladness the Father has in Jesus has been won for us. And because Jesus shares His absolutely pleasing righteousness with me, all those other blessings – the beauty of nature and the richness of food and the preciousness of friendships – are no longer reminders of my lack of gratitude and cold heart, but rather they just pile high as monuments to the abundance of God's inexplicable generosity!

Every gift comes to me through Jesus: above all, His belovedness. Yes, He shares in my gladness, but He also invites me to share in His.

Rejoice in the Lord always; again I will say, rejoice! (Phil. 4:4)

Jesus, You are the joy of the Father! And because of that, His joy in You is ours! Thank you for sharing our gladness, and thank You that You invite us to share Yours too. Give us hearts to receive it today. Amen.

DAY 21: SILENTLY, THE WONDROUS GIFT IS GIVEN

JESUS: SILENT SAVIOUR

Read: Matthew 13:31-32

This season can be so noisy. There are crackers and pantomimes and those ties covered in snowmen that will sing at you in increasing degrees of off-keyness and adverts that everyone has loud opinions on featuring that folk version of what used to be a normal-sounding song. There are increasingly hideous Christmas jumpers and there's that house on the corner that looks like it has melting neon reindeers all over it and there is tinsel, oh, so much tinsel!

All this is going on over the top of a whole host of other harsh loudness. There's hatred, ignorance, heartbreak, persecution, desperate sickness, violence, war – and then countless, countless words being spoken about each of them. And what we need is Jesus. We need the Word made flesh; Light shining in the darkness; the Truth revealed.

Meanwhile, we sing: how silently, how silently – the wondrous gift is given. Part of me wishes that Jesus had come to earth more loudly. Part of me wishes that it didn't seem, from a worldly perspective, so insignificant.

But the silence of His coming is joyful news. His silence is the laying aside of His glory; it's good news of great joy being secured. Jesus was born to us. Jesus was a child, given to us. He became vulnerable, tiny, dependent – so that He might truly be with us, truly be for us, truly be on our side. His coming seemed quiet because Jesus came to be a light in the grimmest, most brutal, devastating darkness there is. His redemption comes through His embracing of weakness and poverty and danger and rejection and violence and humiliation and shame and death. His redemption comes to us because, when it came, it didn't look like glory; it looked like suffering and death.

Maybe your Christmas will feel like an anti-climax. As you sit around the leftovers of a turkey dinner in a crumpled paper hat, navigating the same old family squabbles, feeling like nothing has changed, remember that Jesus came quietly.

The wondrous gift is given in silence. He came quietly, and seemingly insignificantly, with glory and comfort and noise laid aside – but because He did, the people walking in darkness have seen a great light. He has taken on the quietness of our humanity completely, so that He might represent us perfectly, and give us Light eternally. One day He will come again, and it will not be so quiet. But until then, the kingdom continues to grow quietly – with light shining in dark hearts, one by one by one.

The kingdom of heaven is like a grain of mustard seed that a man took and sowed in his field. It is the smallest of all seeds, but when it has grown it is larger than all the garden plants and becomes a tree, so that the birds of the air come and make nests in its branches. (Matt. 13:31, 32)

King Jesus, would Your kingdom grow today. Amen.

DAY 22: RISEN WITH HEALING IN HIS WINGS

JESUS: DEATH-DEFEATER
Read: 1 Corinthians 15:42-57

Hail the heaven born Prince of Peace,
Hail the Sun of Righteousness!
Light and life to all he brings;
Risen with healing in his wings!
Mild he lays his glory by,
Born that man no more may die.
Born to raise the sons of earth;
Born to give them second birth.
Hark, the herald angels sing:
'Glory to the newborn King!'

These words are probably my favorite words in the whole of Carolsville. Given how long I've spent hanging out downtown there these past few months, this is quite the accolade. I love how Wesley so beautifully articulates the link between the birth of Jesus and His resurrection; he sees how fundamentally they are connected, and not only does he know it, but his knowledge erupts into poetic praise!

Yes, Jesus was born to die. He was born as a human to redeem humans, and every minute He lived, He lived so that, at the cross, His innocence could be substituted for my guilt. His birth set Him on the road toward the cross. But He was also born to be raised from the dead. In Bethlehem, it was glory, not the grave that was His goal. And gloriously, He was raised as the firstborn among the dead. First implies that others will follow: and that, among others, is us!

In 1 Corinthians 15, Paul explains how Jesus is a glorious representative of mankind, where the rest of humanity, epitomized by Adam, fell short. I often feel my life is characterized by my connection to the man of dust. I bear the likeness of my forefather: weak, perishable, dishonorable. I feel subject to toil and frustration and death.

But Jesus is born so that, just as we have borne the likeness of the man of dust, we might also bear the likeness of Him, the man from heaven. Jesus came to a world that was under a curse, and lived under a curse, and died under a curse. In embracing the curse, He defeated it. He plumbed the depths of our God-rejecting, futility-ridden, death-destined existence and became a curse for us, for our redemption. He mildly 'laid his glory by' and came right down to meet us in our degradation and shame. He became a son of earth with us and experienced our death for us.

And then, like a phoenix from the ashes, Jesus was raised. On a specific morning in history, Jesus walked out of an actual tomb; on a specific morning in history, He defeated death. After the darkest of nights, the Sun of Righteousness rose. As dawn broke, light and life touched everything on the surface of the earth: there is healing in His wings.

He became a son of earth with us, and endured the worst that earth has to offer, so that we might become a son of heaven with Him – and enjoy the best that heaven has to offer. At Christmas, we celebrate both that Jesus united Himself to us in our death and darkness, and that Jesus has united us to Himself in His all-conquering life and light. And so: joyful all ye nations rise; join the triumph of the skies!

Just as we have borne the image of the man of dust, we shall also bear the image of the man of heaven. (1 Cor. 15:49)

Thank You, Jesus, that You were born, and You lived, and You died. And then You rose! This is our hope! Help us to join the triumph of heaven today, celebrating with the angels: You live! You live! Amen.

DAY 23: DEAR DESIRE OF EVERY NATION

JESUS: HOPE OF THE EARTH

Read: Psalm 96

Psalm 96 is a bold call for a diversity of praise: all the earth is called to sing, for the Lord is to be feared above all. All the world, all the peoples, all the seas, all the fields, and all that is within them are called to rejoice in God.

Have you ever watched David Attenborough and been left reeling in wonder? I especially love an ocean documentary. What an incredible (and frankly weird) variety of creatures lurk beneath our planet's surfaces. The heavens, and the earth, and the seas declare the glory of God, and one of the things they declare most clearly is His diverse excellencies. Out there in the seas are flying stingrays, whales, sharks, whale-sharks, shark-whales, morphing fish, shell-cracking fish, neon-fish, see-through-head fish, crowder-fish, loner-fish, lurk-beneath-the-sand-before-executing-you fish (more scientific names exist). Each says, 'Glory to God' in its own way. And Jesus comes to rescue a people from every tribe, tongue and nation, that each might say 'Glory to God' in their own way.

One Christmas Day, my family spent the morning on a red-dirt road in the equatorial December heat, giving out UNHCR food packages to refugees returning from Tanzania, where they had spent the previous years in camps, to Rwanda. Families carried everything they owned in their hands or on their heads, gratefully taking flavorless biscuits that would likely be their only sustenance on their long journeys home. I say 'home', but they were returning to places stained with memories of slaughter: to torched houses, to mass graves, to communities that had been overturned by betrayal and brutality. Even as an eleven-year-old, I was struck by the undeniable injustice of the situation: why should I be able to go home to a warm bed, when they would spend Christmas on the roadside?

As I consider the Christians on that journey, it strikes me that they glorified Jesus in a different way to me, singing different notes to me. As they headed back to a country ravaged by war, trusting in the Lord for grace to forgive and rebuild, trusting that perfect justice would come, they honored Him in ways I cannot.

Every believer glorifies Jesus in a unique way. Some Christians will honour Jesus by resisting the greed of their culture; some will honour Him by relying on Him every day for food to survive. Some will honour Jesus by trusting Him in the day-to-day fearfulness of life in a war zone; some will honor Him by trusting Him in the day-to-day dullness of an unfulfilling job. Some will honor Jesus by embracing the seemingly mundane 'smallness' of motherhood; some will honor Jesus by rejoicing in Him even though they do not have that privilege. All glorify Him, and glorify Him differently, and glorify Him all the more because of those differences. Jesus comes to make every heart sing: the same song of His glory, but each bringing a different tune sounding out unique ways they have enjoyed Him, unique ways they long for Him, unique ways He has redeemed and fulfilled cultures – in places of prosperity and poverty, in times of peace and brutal war.

Jesus is a great God whose glories are best displayed by a multitude!

When Jesus comes again, there will be great singing and gladness among all who hope in Him. There will be countless languages, countless cultures, countless individuals all declaring the worthiness of the Lamb that was slain: and each individual voice will add something new to the chorus – a particular thread to contribute to the glorious whole.

Let everything that has breath, praise the LORD! Praise the LORD! (Ps. 150:6)

Father God, help me to honor Jesus today – in my unique way, as part of a glorious whole. Amen.

DAY 24: HE SHALL REIGN FOREVER AND EVER

JESUS: ETERNAL KING

Read: Isaiah 65:17-25

Jesus will reign forever. That's the incredible promise of Isaiah 9: 'The increase of his government and peace will have no end.'

'Have Yourself a Merry Little Christmas' has a wistful line in it: 'From now on, our troubles will be out of sight.' I hear that line and my heart swells and yearns with longing: troubles can seem so very present, and so very long lasting. Our burdens can seem stark and harsh and weighty: war and injustice and frustration and the whole world is groaning.

Yes, there are joys – there's the King's strengthening, there's His kingdom growing, there are ways His justice and grace and humility are triumphing in the world. And these are glorious reasons for joy.

But I don't think I feel that my troubles are out of sight. Maybe slightly less in focus? But not out of sight.

Advent reminds us that we're waiting. There is an event in our future that is an eternity-defining moment. As eternity-defining as the moment Heaven's Beloved became a newborn King: Jesus is coming again. He is on the throne now – but the power and influence of His reign will go on forever and ever. There will be a time when He returns, a time when He will wipe away every tear from our eyes. Hallelujah!

But there will be more than that moment of comfort. When a woman is pregnant and waiting, she is not just waiting for the birth day. Of course, there will be excitement and drama and enormous change and relief in the moment the labour pains end, but the birth day is not the end of the story. After the birth day there are other birthdays, there are first burp days and first smile days and first step days and first word days and first schooldays and so on and so on.

Similarly, the whole earth is groaning with birth pangs. But we're not just waiting for the moment when the birth pangs end. We're not just looking forward to the day Jesus returns, but to His reign: an eternal reign. We're looking forward to a new creation that is rich in all those things that fill our hearts with hope and yearning now: rich in diversity, in music, in climate and landscape, in health and happiness. There will be a new creation tended to by the Ultimate Gardener, who is, even now, in the process of pruning and cherishing every new creation in His garden, including you and me. We're looking forward to an eternity of His perfect reign, of justice and peace and creativity and kindness and love and joy. The King will rule, but He will be with us. He will know us, and we will know Him. The joy and love between groom and bride will be delightful and eternal and interesting and glorious – and it will go on increasing in all these ways forever. We're looking forward to future when the troubles of today, of this life, will be truly out of sight. There will be an eternity of peace and prosperity beyond our fathoming, fruitfulness and feasting beyond all comparison, and our troubles will be so far behind us that they won't come to mind.

Jesus' reign has begun already, and we're looking forward to the day when the whole earth will see Him and bow the knee. But we're looking forward to an eternity with Him, beyond that: and the increase of His government and peace will continue forever and ever.

To him who sits on the throne and to the Lamb, be blessing and honor and glory and might forever and ever! (Rev. 5:13)

Thank You, Jesus, that our light and momentary troubles are not worth comparing with the glories of eternity. Help us believe it, whatever today holds. Amen.

DAY 25: UNTO US A CHILD IS BORN

JESUS: GOD'S GIFT

Read: Romans 8:31-39

Happy Christmas to you! We've made it to the end of our 'Preparing for Christmas' journey. And what a joy it's been! As I've written these devotions, I've thought about Jesus and reflected on His kingship and His kindness, His wisdom and His willingness to become weak, His truth and His tenderness, and my heart has so often leaped with hope and joy and praise.

You may have already started opening your presents, or you may, like me, be part of a family that doesn't get going for quite some time. But today's devotion is about the greatest gift you will ever get. It also happens to be a truth that has made the biggest pastoral difference to my Christian walk my whole life long: He is given to us.

He who did not spare his own Son, but gave him up for us all, how will he not also, with Him, graciously give us all things? (Rom. 8:32)

This verse is made up of two parts. A question (how will He not give us all things?) and a statement that is so glorious it takes God's Spirit to carry it to our hearts: God gave us Christ. Unto us a child is born!

All that Jesus is, in His power and mercy and creativity and beauty and boldness and joy and justice and so much more is given to us by the Father. They are not just beautiful qualities; they are ours because we have been united to Him. All that I am is relevant to Jesus. And all that He is, is relevant to me. I have been united with Him.

This means that all that we've pondered and rejoiced over because of Jesus during advent we can delight in afresh in the knowledge that this Christ has been given to us. A child born to us, given to us! And His Name shall be called: Wonderful Counsellor! Almighty God! Everlasting Father! The Prince of Peace!

Nothing can separate us from the love of Christ: not death, nor life, nor angels, nor demons, nor things in the present, nor things to come, nor powers, nor height, nor depth, nor depression, nor singleness, nor loneliness, nor unemployment, nor cancer, nor doubt, nor fear, nor relational breakdown nor (in case anyone is still unsure, Paul spells it out for us here) ANYTHING ELSE IN ALL CREATION. No! We are more than conquerors because He loved us! I am my beloved's, and He is mine!

I don't know what you want most this Christmas. I know that often, at Christmas, our hearts can yearn with longing and nostalgia, with hopes and heartbreak. But I also know that the Word made flesh is the greatest act of generosity in the history of mankind; unto us a child is born, unto us a child is given.

Christian, God's gift to you is Christ: the Christ who is all those things our hearts have rejoiced in this advent: Christ the King, Christ the Little Lord Jesus, Christ the Song of the Angels, Christ the Manger-Messiah, Christ the Grave-Conqueror, Christ the Hope of the Nations, Christ whom the world has insufficient books to adequately describe: this Christ is given to us. To you. Whatever is not mine this Christmas, there is a mighty and glorious reason to rejoice in what has been given to me. His name is Jesus, and nothing in all creation will be able to separate me from His love.

I am my beloved's, and my beloved is mine. (Songs 6:3)

Father God, thank You for not withholding Jesus. Thank You so much that I am His, and He is mine. Amen.

PART TWO

PREPARING FOR THE NEW YEAR

DAY 26: DAILY STOCKINGS

JESUS AND BIBLE READING
Read: Psalm 19

Since I started regular devotions, there have been few things that have done me as much lasting and life-changing good as spending time alone, reading the Bible and praying. And yet, my Quiet Times can still lack discipline, consistency, and at times even existence. It's about this time every year that, once again, I decide to recommit.

I've been trying to understand why. I have many excuses: that I'm tired, that I'm busy, that I have plenty of time so will do it later, that I don't want to be legalistic about Quiet Times or that I won't do a good enough job anyway, so I should just go back to my doom-scrolling.

It struck me afresh the other day that, without realizing it, I was living as though daily devotions are a service I do for God. The word 'devotions' itself seems to imply that it's about how I show my commitment to the Lord. I may know that I read the Bible as a grateful response to having received God's favour, rather than as a way of earning it ('I'm not a

Pharisee!'), but my response remains the point. Will I adequately express my gratitude?

Thankfully, the Bible is not given to us that we might show God our goodness, but that He might show us His. I've not come to the Bible to show my steadfast love, but to *receive* steadfast love.

The Bible is a means by which God gives Himself to me, rather than me to Him. So, when I read the Scriptures, it *is* a reminder of devotion; the Lord's devotion … to me!

Through the Bible, the Lord revives the soul, gives wisdom and joy, brings enlightenment and, take Psalm 119's word for it, so much more! Devotions are not a work, but an act of faith. It's me going to a generous Father with empty hands open to receive from Him. The cure for, 'I don't want to be legalistic about Bible reading' is not less of it, but more, for in God's Word we find Jehovah Jireh revealed: our Provider.

Now, daily times with God don't always feel like I've been given a gift. Sometimes they do. Sometimes, God gives me ointment for a wound, a shield for the day's attack, a wise word for a friend, a sword to cut through entangling lies, a torch for dark days ahead. And I feel it! But sometimes, it feels like I've been given nothing more exciting than a brick.

But those days and weeks where it seems as though I've only gained a boring brick, have piled up to be a monument to remind me, when the storm comes, that God is my refuge and my strength. In trying times, I won't be protected by my knowledge of the Bible; I'll be protected by Jesus. But in the tempest, I will have a monument-reminder of who Jesus is: protector, provider, perfector of my faith.

I've tried to start thinking about my Quiet Times as Gift Times: they are a daily stocking! No child I know skulks in bed on Christmas morning because they don't think they'll do a 'good enough' job of opening their stocking. If they do, there's something not right. Either they have demanding and distant parents or they've completely misunderstood the purpose of stockings and the generosity of their parents' love.

Of course, a chuffed child looking at her brand-new sheep socks, or magic beans, or satsumas or iPhone (modern kids!) may overflow with love and delight in the Giver – but the stocking opening is about their receiving, above all else. And so, with my Quiet Times, I may love Him, and grow in devotion to Him, but it's always going to be because He loved me first.

The life I now live in the flesh I live by faith in the Son of God, who loved me and gave himself for me. (Gal. 2:20)

Father God, in the year ahead, may I learn to receive from You. May I open my heart to You, confident that You will fill it. Amen.

DAY 27: JANUARY LOOMING

JESUS AND DREAD

Read: Matthew 6:25-34

January. Ew.

I know I already wrote off November, so I'm probably sounding a little pessimistic here, but if I were an optimist, I'd probably not mind January either. I'd be better able to see it as an opportunity to shake off the cobwebs of the past year, gird my loins and write (and then complete!) a list of all the ways I intend to be freshly fantastic in the New Year. If I were an optimist, I'd be able to look down the barrel of another year (perhaps using a more optimistic metaphor) and delight in all that lies ahead – undiscovered wonders, unexpected blessings, unprecedented organization.

However, I am no optimist.

January, as far as I can work out, is this wet, cold, drizzly slap in the face, reminding you that not only is Christmas over, but that the post-Christmas period in which you convinced yourself you'd become the ideal version of yourself is also over. With my non-optimistic bent, I don't tend to look to the future with hope. I tend to be afraid. I worry that my life might be inadequate. I worry either that something terrible will happen, or if it doesn't, nothing good will happen. January lurks menacingly at the end of the year. It's coming to ask me what's new, what I've achieved, how my character is growing, how I'm *really* doing… and I'm going to want to slap January back in its wet, cold, drizzly face.

As I await January then, I am so thankful for these words from Jesus in Matthew 6: 'Your heavenly Father knows what you need.' There is so much that I am inclined to worry about. But Jesus says: Don't worry, because your heavenly Father knows what you need. He is attentive to you. He cares about you. He loves you with an everlasting love. He knows what you need.

And Jesus says, 'Seek first the kingdom of God, and his righteousness, and all these things will be added to you.' The logic is: don't make yourself your primary concern. Your heavenly Father has got your back. In all those scenarios you anticipate with fear, He knows what you need. Even when you haven't begun to figure out exactly what it is you need, He knows. Lift your eyes up, away from the darkness that lurks within you, up from the fog that clouds the path ahead, and look to the righteousness of God. Jesus says, you can trust the Father, and He knows Him better than anyone else. He knows what it is to entrust Himself to God when there is no future and no hope without Him.

'Your heavenly Father knows what you need' are words to liberate us from worry, but also to liberate us from ourselves! If my heavenly Father knows what I need, then I need not be my primary concern. Knowing that my needs are met, I can love my neighbour. Knowing my needs are met, I can make His kingdom the focus of the year to come.

Beloved, if God so loved us, we ought to love one another. (1 John 4: 11)

Father God, I don't know what will lie ahead in the New Year. But You gave Your Son to meet my greatest need, to be my identity and strong tower, and You know what I need. Thank You. Amen.

DAY 28: PRESENT TENSE HOPEFULNESS

JESUS AND WAITING

Read: Psalm 146

There's nothing like 'Twixtmass' to make you feel like you are living in some alternate time zone. Yes, you are here, but you aren't completely sure where 'here' is: is it the weekend? Is it a Tuesday? How many days are left until January and what year is ending anyway? It's a season that can sometimes feel like a 'no-man's land' of waiting for something to happen.

Sometimes, I find Christian living can feel similar. I know that Jesus came, and it was fantastic, and I know that one day He will come again, and act decisively, swallowing up death and sin and darkness. All that has been sown in dishonor, weakness, and death will be raised, in glory, in power, in immortality. What hope! But what about now? Are we just in a 'no-man's land', waiting for something to happen?

The problem with this thinking is that it means I tend to see God as being aloof, or quiet, or, for the time being, passive. This is a gross underestimation of the Sustainer of the Universe! Re-reading some of the psalms recently, I was reminded of these amazing words of Jesus: '*my Father is always at work… and I too am working*' (John 5:17 NIV).

The psalmists look to the future with great hope and joy, but their hope in God is also in the present tense. It's a joyful reminder to me of the truth about the Lord; He is not distant, but attentive. He is not passive, but active.

As I read the Psalms I am moved by the intent tenderness of God. Rather than painting a picture of a far-off, hardened, impersonal deity, the psalms testify to a kind, merciful, star-making, yet profoundly personal covenant Lord, who takes attentive, affectionate care of His people.

He delivers, He shelters, He shields with faithfulness. He commands angels concerning those who take refuge in Him, He protects, He hears prayers: He answers! He accompanies those in trouble, He rescues, honours, satisfies, and upholds. The Lord shows His salvation: He forms, He leads, He hems in, He upholds. The Lord is a Shepherd among His people; He restores, He comforts, He prepares, He anoints. He surrounds and heals and redeems and crowns with steadfast love and mercy.

Yes, many of these things will be finally and decisively fulfilled with the return of Christ. But the Lord is at work now. He is doing these things now. He is actively at work for good in all things now.

The Lord is working righteousness for the oppressed: He's making known His ways. He's showing compassion, executing justice, setting prisoners free. He's opening blind eyes, He's lifting up the bowed down, He's binding up broken hearts, He's watching over the sojourners, He's upholding the widows and the fatherless. He's exalting the humble, and He's bringing the way of the wicked to ruin.

When life feels like Twixtmass, when I feel like God is passive, it helps to say to myself: Look! Look at the psalms! Look at the wealth of His activity! Yes, I take refuge in Him, but He is not a passive shelter. I hold fast to Him, and He holds fast to me. Yes, I long for His return. I long for His reign of righteousness and goodness and power. And as I long, I wait, thankful for the Lord's patience. But the Lord's patience does not mean passivity; in countless and God-glorifying ways, it means salvation.

The Lord's patience means salvation. (2 Pet. 3:9, NIV)

Thank You Father, that You are at work. Even today! Give me eyes to see it, and a heart that delights in it. For Your glory, Amen.

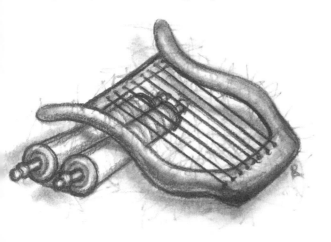

DAY 29: GRAVESIDE

JESUS AND DISAPPOINTMENT
Read: Matthew 16:24-28

Sometimes, looking ahead to a New Year can be painful. I wrote this poem during a time when I was reflecting on how my life hadn't turned out how I had hoped. For you, there may be different dreams and desires that you have had to see die. A New Year seems like a good time to hand those losses over to Jesus, and to say – I trust that You will restore the years the locusts have eaten. I trust that You will be able to bring a great harvest from the death of these seeds in the ground; I trust that You can take my spirit of despair and replace it with the oil of gladness. The Lord knows how to bring life after death. Resurrection is His speciality, after all.

Another trip around the sun,
Another December nearly through – And I'm standing at
my graveside,
Soil in hand,
Staring at the depths

and thinking
R.I.P.

R.I.P the me
Who would have been loved at 23,
R.I.P. the me
Who by now would be a mother of three,
R.I.P the me
Who'd have known community,
Thrived as a missionary,
Been healthy, been happy, been holy – Who'd have been
done with therapy.

I know a man who said that
to really live you need to really die,
That if you want to truly flourish,
It starts with the death of I.

That's why I'm standing at my graveside
Weeping 'R.I.P, me' – Because that man died at thirty three
– Ashes to ashes,
dust to dust,

R.I.P.
A seed that had to perish in the dark,
before it bloomed to glory.

So, another trip around the sun,
Another familiar chill,
And I am standing at my graveside,
Soil in hand,

and saying 'R.I.P me',
but trying to believe.

I'm trying to believe
That growth can come from the barren, frosty earth,
That death and death and death
will eventually give way to birth.

So much of me has died here
Year on year on year,
Of dreams and dread and dread and death,
Of dreams, then dread, then death.
Winter has followed winter,
Who would dare to hope for spring?

Yet I'm standing at my graveside,
And the last of the leaves are swept away
by the bitter, icy breeze,

But I'm still trying to believe,
Even as I grieve,
That one day, 'R.I.P me'
might become a song of resurrection,
A song of victory.

Truly, truly, I say to you, unless a grain of wheat falls to the
earth and dies, it remains alone; but if it dies, it bears much
fruit. (John 12:24)

Risen Jesus, thank You that You know what it is to die. Help us to trust You with our losses and disappointments. Though weeping may last for the night, may Your joy come in the morning. Amen.

DAY 30: WHO AM I?

JESUS AND IDENTITY

Read: Psalm 139

After yesterday's moment to grieve in hope, it feels worth taking today to look to the year ahead and celebrate. So, here are some things that define you more than your current relationship status, your job performance, your CV, your genetics, your appearance, your health, your past, your successes, your failures, whatever might happen in the year to come and pretty much everything else. Hurray!

• you are made in the image of God (Gen. 1:27)

• you are a disciple and a disciple maker (Matt. 28:19)

• you were a lost sheep, and the Creator of the world rejoiced to see you found (Luke 15:7)

• the most authoritative being in the Universe sets you free: you are free indeed (John 8:36)

• your Shepherd laid down his life for you (John 10:11)

• and you are a friend of Jesus (John 15:15)

• your sins will NEVER be counted against you (Rom. 4:7-8)

- you are more than a conqueror through Him who loved you (Rom. 8:37)
- you are a temple of the Holy Spirit (1 Cor. 6:19)
- and you live because another died in your place (1 Cor. 15:3)
- you are being prepared for an almighty and incomparable weight of glory (2 Cor. 4:17)
- you are now the righteousness of God (2 Cor. 5:21)
- you are a true descendent of Abraham (Gal. 3:7)
- you have the Spirit of the Son in your heart (Gal. 4:6)
- so you are no longer a slave (Gal. 4:7)
- you were chosen before time began (Eph. 1:4)
- and you are God's masterpiece, created in Christ Jesus to do good works God prepared for you (Eph. 2:10)
- you are no longer darkness, but light in the Lord (Eph. 5:8)
- you are a citizen of heaven (Phil. 3:20)
- you are completely forgiven (Col. 1:14)
- your life is hidden with Christ in God (Col. 3:3)
- your life IS Christ (Col. 3:4)
- and you will appear with Christ in glory (Col. 3:4)
- you are united to the One who abolished death (2 Tim. 1:10)
- and you are called because of God's purpose and grace (2 Tim. 1:9)
- you are a sibling of Jesus, and He's glad about it (Heb. 2:11)
- you no longer live in fear of death (Heb. 2:15)
- you have a perfect mediator (Heb. 12:24)

- you have an imperishable, undefiled and unfailing inheritance (1 Pet. 1:4)
- you are still chosen (1 Pet. 2:1)
- you have been ransomed by the most precious treasure there is (1 Pet. 1:19)
- you are royal (1 Pet. 2:9)
- and you are part of a priesthood (1 Pet. 2:9)
- you belong to God (1 Pet. 2:9, 1 Cor. 6: 19-20)
- in fact, you are a child of God (1 John 1:3)
- and He has lavished you with love (1 John 3:1)
- you are kept by the One who died in your place (Jude 1)
- you are beloved in God the Father (Jude 1)
- yes, you are loved by Him (Rev. 1:5)

Whatever your status in life, it is not permanent. But something permanent is coming, something weighty and real and full of splendour.

> *Christ loved the church and gave himself up for her, that he might sanctify her, having cleansed her by the washing of water with the word, so that he might present the church to himself in splendour… (Eph. 5:25-27)*

Lord Jesus, thank You so much for the great and precious promises that are mine because You gave them to me! Thank You for who I am in You. May I know You more every day of the year ahead, for the sake of Your glory, Amen.

DAY 31: RESOLUTIONS

JESUS AND THE NEW YEAR
Read: Isaiah 40

Made any resolutions yet? I thought about a few ... thousand. Somewhere in the middle of my list of go-to methods for becoming a better exercised, better read, better disciplined, better fed, altogether more chilled (!) version of myself, I was relieved to remember that my hope for this year is not what I resolve to do or be, but the Lord.

He has made steadfast promises, and His unwavering resolve and delight in keeping them are my brightest hope for the New Year, the reason I can look forward to it with joy.

Here are His resolutions:

I will be with you. Whether this year is better or not, whether you shake free that belligerent, besetting fault or not, whether you make it to the gym or not, whether you feel like I am with you or whether it feels like you are alone, every day and every night of this year, I will be with you.

I will love you. Abundantly, extravagantly, in ways that will stagger and surprise you. However you may love me, be it in blazing flames or as a smoldering wick: I will love you. I will love loving you. Long before you've muttered a prayer or picked up the Bible, long before you've made it to church, long before you even want to love me, every day of this year: I will love you.

I will help you. *When there's nothing left within – look to me: I will help you. When you think you're all over it – look to me: I will help you. When no one else will, or can, I will delight to be your strength and your hope. Every day of this year, I will be your ever-present help in trouble.*

I will forgive you. *I will be faithful and just, and the cross will be enough – for the year's most floundering attempts at goodness and the year's most profound failures. Where resolve doesn't win and instead, greed does or despair does or sloth does or selfishness does, I will remember the cross; I will remember the covenant; I will remember your Mediator, my Beloved Son and, with pleasure, I will forgive you.*

I will give you rest. *I will. As you peer into a frantic New Year where countless demands yap at you to eat less, exercise more, scroll less, read more, introspect less, chill more, as you deeply desire to be a thousand things you are not now, as you try to carve out a peaceful path for yourself in being a better version of you, remember that, whatever your resolutions might give you, I will give you rest.*

I will make all things new. *Tenderly, creatively, redemptively, exhaustively. When you feel like everything is predictable or miserable or futile; when you've tried and tried and feel like all you've made is a mess: I will make all things new. When this year looks like another year heavy with heartache and foolishness and oppression and pain, I will make all things* *new. When the world is breaking, when rulers are raging, when the wounded are weeping, I will be making all things new.*

I will glorify my name by being who I am. I will bind up broken hearts. I will set captives free. I will hear prayers and answer. I will deliver. I will give food to the hungry. I will uphold the cause of the oppressed. I will be faithful because I cannot be anything else. I will love being faithful. I will love being faithful to you.[1]

I don't know what I'll be doing in the New Year, but I know what God will be doing: He has promised. These are the resolutions that matter. These are the resolutions that make for a Happy New Year.

'Have you not known? Have you not heard? The LORD is the everlasting God, the Creator of the ends of the earth. He does not faint or grow weary; his understanding is unsearchable. He gives power to the faint, and to him who has no might he increases strength.' (Isa. 40: 28, 29)

Happy New Year!

Father God, You are our hope for a happy New Year. Give us hearts to see You and trust You. In Jesus' Name, and for His glory. Amen.

---

1   References: Isaiah 43:2; Matthew 28:20; Romans 8:31-39; Isaiah 54:10; Isaiah 41:10; Psalm 46:1; Isaiah 1:18; 1 John 1:9; Matthew 11:28-20; Revelation 21:5; Psalm 146 and many more…

Appendix of Carols

'And Can It Be', Charles Wesley (1738)

'Angels from the Realms of Glory', James Montgomery (1816)

'Away in a Manger', Anonymous (1885)

'Brightest and Best of The Sons of the Morning', Reginold Heber (1811)

'Deck the Halls', Thomas Oliphant (1862)

'Go Tell it On the Mountain', John Wesley Work Jr (1865)
'Hark the Herald Angels Sing!', Charles Wesley (1739)

'In the Bleak Midwinter', Christina Rosetti (1872)
'It Came Upon a Midnight Clear', Edmund Sears (1849)

'Jesus, the Name High Over All', Charles Wesley (1749)

'Joy to the World', Isaac Watts (1719)

'Mary's Boy Child', Jester Hairston (1956)

'O Come, All Ye Faithful', Frederick Oakley, translator (1841)

'O Come, O Come Emmanuel', John Mason Neale, translator (1861)

'O For a Thousand Tongues to Sing', Charles Wesley (1739)

'O Holy Night', John Sullivan Dwight, translator (1847)

'O Little Town of Bethlehem', Philips Brookes (1868)

'Once in Royal David's City', Cecil Frances Alexander (1848)

'Silent Night', Joseph Moer (1833)

'The Hallelujah Chorus', Charles Jennens (1741)

'Unto Us a Child is Born!' Charles Jennens (1741)

'We Three Kings', John Henry Hopkins (1857)

ACKNOWLEDGEMENTS

This book, as it is, would not exist without:

- Rebekah Lesan: thank you so much for your illustrative skill, patience, generosity and faith.
- Carol writers of the past, who helped inspire many of the posts in Part One: what a joy to be able to 'stand on the shoulders' of your wonder!
- Christian Focus. Special thanks to Margaret Roberts, Kate Mackenzie, Maegan Roper, Rosanna Burton, James Amour, Irene Roberts and Anne Norrie.
- Rob, Trish and Tim Wilson, and Jo and Jason Hockley, who gave me the time, space, love and laughter needed for writing to happen.
- Tim and Ollie Hockley, who gave me a proper break when I needed it.
- Ashley Wright, who reminds me of the promise of Psalm 27:13 regularly, and whom God has used to fulfil it more times than I can remember.

- Katie Stileman's weekly doses of hilarity and sanity (one very much supporting the other).
- The Alarcon family, who gave me a place to work on the manuscript while modelling the generosity of the One I was writing about. May this book be a blessing to you, your family, and your church.
- The highs and lows of life as a teacher. Among other things, it gave me the commute where I first began to listen to carols with writing in mind, paid for the time to write, and brought a truck load of wonderful humans into my life! Special thanks to Hannah Boyce for her expert and timely advice.

Like Charles Wesley longing for 999 more tongues to adequately express the glories of Christ, and in the words of S. M. Lockridge in his beautiful 'That's my King' sermon (look it up!), I reach the end of this book about Jesus and my heart cries, 'Oh, I wish I could describe Him to you!' He is all this, and He is so much more, and one day, we will be with Him.

> *'I, Jesus, am the bright morning star.' The Spirit and the bride say, 'come!' … he who testifies to these things says, 'yes, I am coming soon.' (Rev. 22)*

The following is a sample from Philippa Ruth Wilson's first title, *A Certain Brightness: Bible Devotions for Troubled Times*

THE LORD IS MY SHEPHERD

PSALM 23:1

And I am a sheep.

By which I mean that I am weak, vulnerable and foolish. These things together make a terrible combination, and can make hard times feel complicated: am I suffering because of my weakness? My bad choices? Someone else's bad choices? Because the world in general is terribly broken?

Thankfully, God refers to us as sheep and acknowledges our need for a shepherd. He knows that we are complex and that some of our problems come from our defencelessness against wolves, some from our bad choices to wander off sheer cliff faces, and some from our circumstances (we were born with a certain disposition or a certain lack of wool). Without taking the metaphor any further, the point stands: we are like sheep, a mixture of being weak, vulnerable and foolish.

But the Lord is my shepherd. And this is wonderful news, because He does not respond to my sheepishness, with anger or with disappointment, but by meeting my needs. By being the Good Shepherd.

Across the Scriptures[1] we are assured:

- I am selfish; He lays down His life for mine. I am confused; He knows me thoroughly.
- I am exposed; He brings me into His fold. I am fearful; He speaks comfort.
- I am wayward; He pursues me until He has brought me home. I fear repentance; He rejoices to find me.
- I can't make my own way back; He carries me home and rejoices on the journey.
- I am weary; He gathers me in His arms.
- I am uncertain; He leads me in paths of righteousness.
- I am surrounded by enemies; He makes me a feast in their presence.
- I let Him down; He restores me.
- In my weakness He is strong; in my vulnerability He is tender.
- In my foolishness He is wise; in my helplessness He is my refuge.

We are a strange mixture of weakness and uncertainty and sinfulness, and it can be exhausting trying to parse it all out. But the Lord is sufficient for all our nuances: our psychology, our circumstances, our character flaws and our natural frailty. He delights to gather the whole bundle of our sheepishness in His arms, and carry us close to His heart (Isa. 40:11).

---

1   Based on: Psalm 23, Psalm 100, Isaiah 40, Luke 15, John 10, and Colossians.

The LORD is my shepherd, I have everything I need (Ps. 23:1).

Jesus, my Shepherd, thank You that Your goodness and mercy will be with me every day of my life, and on into eternity. Help me to believe it, amid fear and uncertainty and weakness. Let me know Your goodness as the Shepherd who has laid down His life for me, and may I know Your voice. For Your sake, Amen.

I was lost, but Jesus found me,
Found the sheep that went astray,
Threw His loving arms around me,
Drew me back into His way.

Days of darkness still come o'er me,
Sorrow's path I often tread,
But His presence still is with me;
By His guiding hand I'm led.
F. H. Rowley (1854–1952)

A Certain Brightness

Bible Devotions for Troubled Times

Philippa Ruth Wilson

A Certain Brightness

Bible Devotions for Troubled Times

PHILIPPA RUTH WILSON

The devotions in this book are short, encouraging, and a reminder of the light when everything seems dark. Philippa Wilson has begun each chapter with a five–word Bible phrase that is easily memorised and ended with a prayer. Beautiful illustrations by Rebekah Lesan make this an ideal book to give to friends who are struggling.

This is a lovely book. Pastoral, sensitive and full of wisdom, it offers comfort and companionship to those who are struggling. I've been blessed and encouraged by it. I am thankful to Philippa for sharing from her own experiences and for reminding me of the God who shines brightest in the dark.

Emma Scrivener
Blogger at emmascrivener.net and author of *A New Name* and *A New Day*

In the darkest of days, sometimes all we can consume is a few morsels at a time. A Certain Brightness *provides just that – morsels of gospel truth. This devotional is written for the weary and down–trodden. It is a gentle and quiet whisper that cuts into the cacophony of our minds, reminding us of the One who loves us most.*

Christina Fox
Counselor, retreat speaker and author

978-1-5271-0691-8

Also available from Christian Focus Publications…

God's Spirit
The Antidote to Chaos

Reuben Hunter

God's Spirit

The Antidote to Chaos

Reuben Hunter

To live well in this world, we need more than to just try harder. If we want lives that are marked by love, joy and peace, if we want to see goodness planted in the soil of our marriages and families, we need something we can't actually drum up from inside ourselves, however hard we try or how disciplined we become. The truth is, we need someone to come from outside of us to empower us to live the good life. But He doesn't just say try harder, He comes to us in the person of His Spirit, to enable us to grow into those people, to more closely resemble His Son, the Lord Jesus.

A gem of a little book, at the same time wonderfully encouraging and profoundly challenging. ... a counter–cultural call which offers not only transformation for us as individuals, but for our relationships, and for our society. Recommended.

Daniel Strange
College Director, Oak Hill Theological College, London

... allows divine truth to speak to human struggle, showing us how God's people are called and enabled to live counter–cultural lives before a watching world and to the glory of God. I highly recommend it.

Tony Merida
Pastor, Imago Dei Church, Raleigh, North Carolina and author
of *Love Your Church*

978-1-5271-0839-4

Christian Focus Publications

Our mission statement —

STAYING FAITHFUL

In dependence upon God we seek to impact the world through literature faithful to His infallible Word, the Bible. Our aim is to ensure that the Lord Jesus Christ is presented as the only hope to obtain forgiveness of sin, live a useful life and look forward to heaven with Him.

Our books are published in four imprints:

CHRISTIAN FOCUS

Popular works including biographies, commentaries, basic doctrine and Christian living.

CHRISTIAN HERITAGE

Books representing some of the best material from the rich heritage of the church.

MENTOR

Books written at a level suitable for Bible College and seminary students, pastors, and other serious readers. The imprint includes commentaries, doctrinal studies, examination of current issues and church history.

CF4•K

Children's books for quality Bible teaching and for all age groups: Sunday school curriculum, puzzle and activity books; personal and family devotional titles, biographies and inspirational stories — because you are never too young to know Jesus!

Christian Focus Publications Ltd,
Geanies House, Fearn, Ross-shire,
IV20 1TW, Scotland, United Kingdom.
www.christianfocus.com